THE *Cradle* THAT WAITS

THE Cradle THAT WAITS

A Woman's Journey with Infertility, Miscarriage, and Faith

JUDINE GORDON

CONCLUSIO
HOUSE PUBLISHING

Copyright © 2016 by Judine Gordon

All rights reserved. This book or any portion thereof may not be reproduced or used in any manner whatsoever without the express written permission of the publisher except for the use of brief quotations in a book review.

"The Cradle That Waits: A Woman's Journey with Infertility, Miscarriage, and Faith"

Printed in Canada
First Printing, 2016

ISBN 978-0-9949204-5-4

Published by:
Conclusio House Publishing
503-7700 Hurontario Street
Suite 209
Brampton, ON, L6Y 4M3
www.conclusiohouse.com

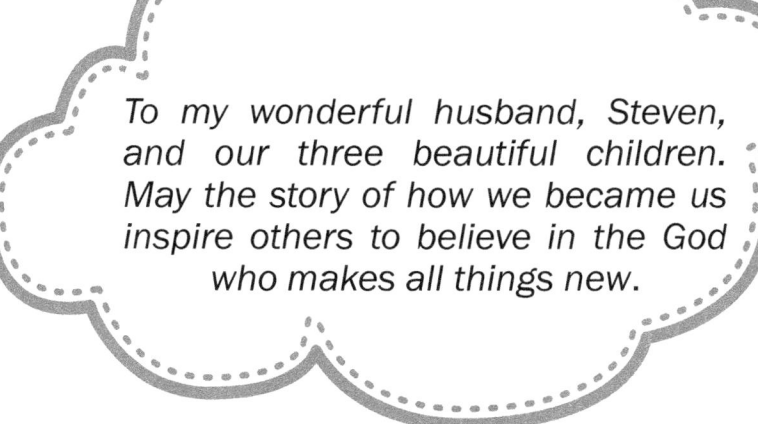

To my wonderful husband, Steven, and our three beautiful children. May the story of how we became us inspire others to believe in the God who makes all things new.

Acknowledgements

I would like to thank, from the bottom of my heart, our parents and family, whose continuous support and encouragement helped get us through a very tough time in our lives, and whose unconditional love for our kids is irreplaceable.

To my mother and mother-in-law, your love carries me daily. I love you both so very much.

I would like to extend my sincerest and heartfelt gratitude to Pastor Orim Meikle and Pastor Judith Meikle. Without your constant prayers, we might not be where we are today. We love you and we thank you for never giving up!

To the following people whose friendship, love, and prayers helped to carry me when I felt like giving up: Maxine Campbell, Moheen Lombard, Lisa Patrick, Nicole Mitchell, Liny Antwi, Rochelle Brissett, Tamara and Dominic Nti, Keisha-Ann Carter, Sherene and Peter Isaac. Thank you all so much!

To Sarah Zaman and Maninder Athwal, you ladies are the best! Thank you both for always being there and for keeping me smiling.

To Kerri-Ann Haye-Donawa, this would not be possible without you! Thank you for answering the call of God on your life.

To the staff and parents at the Village Montessori School, thank you all for your positive words and encouragement; it meant so much.

To the many people who prayed for us and offered words of encouragement, thank you!

Thank you to my Lord and Saviour Jesus Christ, with whom all things are possible!

Table of Contents

Preface	xi
Chapter One	1
Chapter Two	10
Chapter Three	17
Chapter Four	23
Chapter Five	31
Chapter Six	41
Chapter Seven	52
Chapter Eight	62
Chapter Nine	69
Chapter Ten	73
Epilogue	76
A Prayer for your womb	79

Preface

When I was growing up, I never gave much thought to the concept of getting pregnant. Now, when I say *getting pregnant*, I don't mean having sex; that's the easy part. I mean what happens inside of my body after the sex is over—the *getting pregnant*. Throughout my youth, adults made it sound as though one kiss would impregnate me for sure. And if I had sex, well then I would end up as a single mother, on welfare, with a boatload of kids trailing behind me. It was just that easy to get pregnant!

Now that I'm older and trying to get pregnant, I have come to realize that it really isn't as easy as it sounds. If you are reading this book then chances are you can identify with my struggle. For the past few years I have looked at every pregnant woman I see with new and wondering eyes. With each one that I see, new questions fill my heart, like *Why was it so easy for you? What did you do differently? What have you got that I don't? Why is your baby growing healthy and strong, when I had to watch mine bleed out after only a few weeks? Why did my baby have to die?*

It was only after my second pregnancy loss that I took a deeper look into pregnancy, how it happens, and what happens if it doesn't happen. Let me tell you, it is not as easy as they made it sound. Even after my miscarriage, people who heard about it still made pregnancy seem easy. I heard so many comments like, "Don't worry, you can have another one," or "You're lucky it happened early," or "You're going to be pregnant again before you know it!" Those people had no idea the profound impact those statements had on me, and how negatively they affected my healing process. Not that those statements weren't true, but having another child would never replace the one I had lost and, no, I did not feel lucky that it happened early, when I was so sad that it had happened at all. And as for getting pregnant again? How could I go into another pregnancy with the same innocence as the first, believing that everything would go as planned like I had always been told? I couldn't. Not after what happened. Because things don't always go as planned, and you really have no control over how things do go.

One person in particular solidified these fears with a story she must have thought would've given me hope. "I know someone who had *seven* miscarriages before having her first child!" she said. How could this story be helpful? Did that mean that I might have to endure this agony six more times before I would get my baby? I truly wished that she had kept this story to herself, for she had placed a new fear in my heart. *What if this does happen again? What if this keeps happening?*

I also found that after such a loss, I could no longer find comfort in all of my usual places. It was hard for me to discuss what I was going through with my husband, who is usually the person I discuss all of my struggles with. Sure, he was there to listen and he helped me out in any way he could, but, being a man, he could never fully comprehend how this loss had affected me. There were many times when I prayed that God would help me to be able to move on, but even prayer seemed futile, because my faith in God had taken such a hard hit. Before my pregnancy losses, I just assumed that because I was a Christian God had my back and would ensure that I had a healthy baby. I was convinced that as long as I "declared" a healthy pregnancy, I would have one. Now I know better. I spent many months feeling so betrayed by God that even praying seemed out of the question. I felt like an alien in church, because everyone else seemed to have such confidence that God was fighting their battles for them, while I felt so alone in mine. I kept wondering, *What's the point of praying if God is just going to turn His back and do His own thing anyway?* I had so many questions with no one to answer any of them, and the worst part was that I felt like a huge sinner just for asking these questions. Sometimes people make it seem like God is not to be questioned; we are just supposed to trust that He knows what He is doing and go along for the ride. Well, I can now say that this experience has introduced me to a whole new God! Not some genie in a bottle who just gives His children whatever they ask for, or some cruel God that just does things and expects us to keep our mouths shut about it. This God allows us to ask questions and wonder why. This God understands that bad things can, and frequently do, happen but He is always there to help us through them. Don't get me wrong, this is the same God as before. It is simply my understanding of Him that has changed.

To be honest, I am not quite sure how to begin this book. All I can say is that I never gave much thought to pregnancy loss. I really never thought that I would go through such a thing, because, quite simply, I never thought that I deserved such a thing. I know it sounds naive, and it is. It is only now that I have taken the time out to truly realize that, in this world, we just don't always get what we deserve. In fact, Christian or not, bad things often happen.

All too often, Christians are taught to believe that, as children of God, we are entitled to a struggle-free life. If we are going through a hard time, then we must declare and pray ourselves out of it. On the other hand, some are taught that God is not to be questioned, and we must just carry the load that we are meant to carry. He carried His cross, and so we must carry ours without complaint. Even women who are of a different faith have been taught that if they think positive thoughts, then positive things will come their way. While these beliefs are great when things are going well, they can become very discouraging when, despite how positive your thoughts are, bad things just keep happening. We are left wondering, *Why isn't it working?*

I am writing this book, not for myself, but for

you, the woman reading this book who is going through the "ttc struggle"—trying to conceive. I am writing this so that you will be patient with others when they say things like, "One day you will forget all about this." They just don't understand. They can't understand. I am writing this book so that, in the midst of this hard time, you will know that someone does understand. I am the person who can honestly say, "I understand." I am the person walking with you when you feel alone in your loss. I am the person sitting silently beside you when you don't want to talk, but you still want to be heard. I just want you to know that everything you're feeling is normal. The questions you're asking are okay. I am hoping to enable you to feel free to *feel*, to question, to wonder, to grieve, to hope, to doubt, to believe.

Praying your cradle will be filled,
Judine Gordon

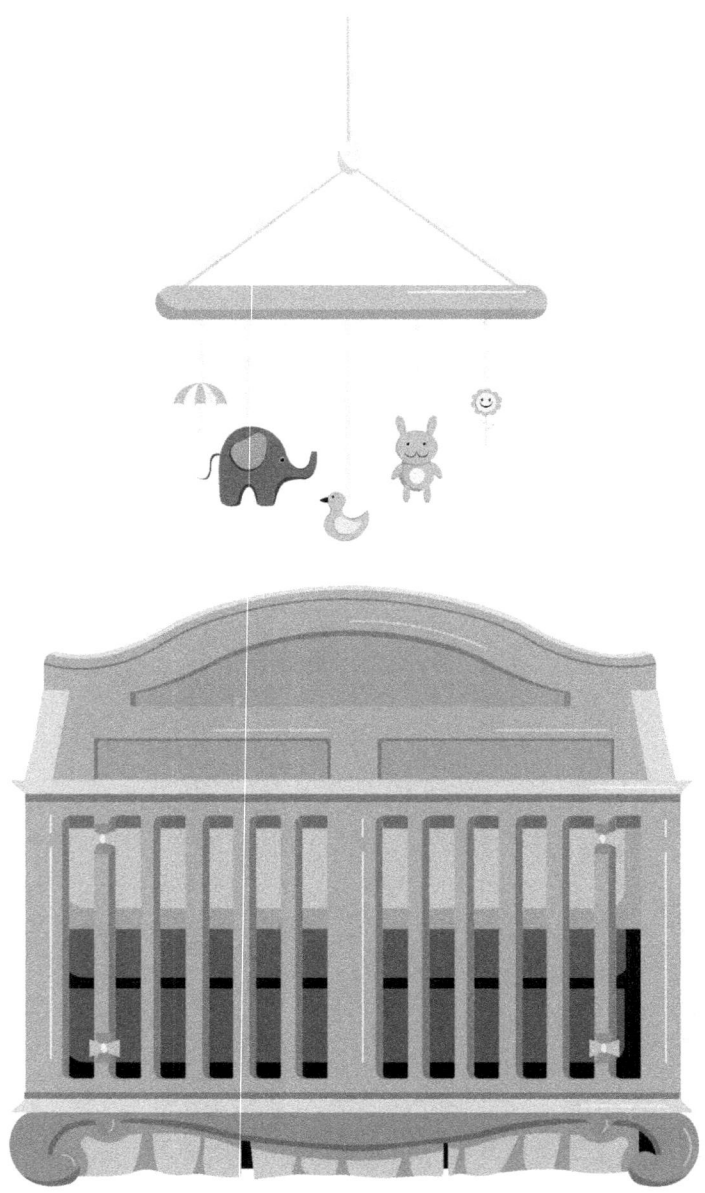

Chapter 1

The first time I got pregnant was just about two and a half months after my husband and I got married. We were a little surprised to get pregnant so soon, but we couldn't have been happier. I prayed more during that short time than I ever had before. You see, whenever I prayed, I tried my best not to ask for things. I believed that whatever I needed God had already supplied, and so in thanking Him, I was constantly reminding myself that He is able and willing to provide for me. This was the first time in a long time that I had really asked God for anything.

When I was just a little girl, my favourite game to play was always '*House*.' I had loved to read the series 'Sweet Valley Twins', and would often pretend that I had identical twin girls myself. I loved playing the mom. I wanted to grow up and have a family of my own. I once wrote a journal entry stating that when I grew up I wanted to have a boy and identical twin girls, just like in the Sweet Valley books. I always knew that I wanted to be a mom. I was so happy about my pregnancy that while I drove to work every morning I asked God to protect my baby and to bless me with a healthy pregnancy. I prayed against any and every birth defect I could think of. I prayed against every single learning, social, emotional, physical, and mental disability as well. I even prayed against miscarriage. However, despite my fervent prayers, a few days after the positive pregnancy test, I miscarried. It happened one evening after work while my husband and I were eating dinner. I excused myself to go to the bathroom and noticed that I had some spotting. I told my husband that it was probably nothing to worry about, but we should go to the hospital anyway, just to make sure. At the hospital, a blood test revealed that I was having a miscarriage. I will never forget how casually the nurse exclaimed, "It doesn't look like this one will make it. But not to worry, you'll be pregnant again before you know it!" *How could he be so nonchalant about the death of a child? My child!*

Although I was sad, I tried not to get discouraged. I told myself that this must have been a fluke. It was just one of those things, and I refused to question whether God had actually heard all of my prayers or not. I didn't want this 'episode' to cause me to question my faith, and I was eager to try again right away, positive that I would go on to have a healthy and successful pregnancy. In fact, I was so eager that I completely ignored the doctor's orders to wait at least three months before trying again. Three months, he said, would give my body, as well as my heart, time to heal. I remember coming home from that appointment and my husband asking me when the doctor said we could try again. I told him that the doctor said there was no need to wait. I lied. After all, there were tons of stories online of women who miscarried, got pregnant right away, and carried healthy babies to term. I was determined to be one of those ladies. And all of the research showed that women were very fertile after a pregnancy loss. I didn't want to miss my window. So I lied.

Today I am ashamed of my behaviour, but at the time I was desperately trying to hold on to a child that we had already lost. I guess I thought that if I were pregnant again, it would seem like the miscarriage hadn't happened. Like I had been pregnant all along and could carry on living as though nothing had happened at all. All I could think about for the two weeks following the miscarriage was ovulation and "timing things right." That first pregnancy slipped away too easily from my grip, and I would have done anything to be pregnant, again. I would never have imagined that the two years following that first miscarriage were possible for me. I really believed with all of my heart that because I didn't 'deserve' it, it wouldn't happen again.

If you're reading this book, then I'm sure you've already figured out that 'deserving' has nothing to do with it. In fact, if I had been paying attention at the time, I would have noticed then that there are so many deserving people without children, and much more undeserving people with children. And if we all got what we deserved, then life would be so much more predictable, comfortable, and fair.

So with this naive understanding, I rushed to try again, already naming this child that I was sure to conceive. I happily browsed the baby section in the store as I waited until the day my ovulation kit told me that it was time. I laughed with excitement when that time came, and set the mood with rose petals, lingerie, and music. I waited impatiently for the two weeks to pass so I could take a pregnancy test, and all the while I continued to plan for this baby that I was certain was on its way. I still found it difficult to see pregnant women at church or in the malls, but I kept telling myself, "That's going to be you soon."

I struggled daily to ignore the one truth that was eating away at my heart—my baby had died. Even if I got pregnant again this time, I could never undo what had happened. I knew that my next pregnancy would be fraught with uncertainty, worry, and fear. Aside from counting the days to ovulation, I was also painfully aware of the passing weeks and kept mental track of how far along I would have been if my baby had lived. May 25th was the due date in that pregnancy, and so every year on this date I still remember and wonder what life would have been like if I had gotten the chance to meet that child. That's the hardest thing about pregnancy loss, you never forget. Yes, you will heal, but you'll never be the same. Regardless of how early on the loss happened, that was *your* baby. Every day I had to tell myself to stay positive and move on.

So, pushing these thoughts aside, I waited for the right time to take a pregnancy test. However, instead of the positive pregnancy test that I was waiting for, I was met with another harsh reality. One afternoon, while I was in my classroom, surrounded by students, I began to have excruciating abdominal pains. They came on so suddenly that I thought it had to be my appendix. Terrified, I called another teacher to take over my class and immediately left for home. I called my husband on the way, and he left work to meet me there. But by the time I got home, I could barely make it up the stairs to my room. I desperately called my mother-in-law, who lived five minutes away, to take me to the hospital. You know, it's funny the things that cross your mind at the most inappropriate times. In the midst of all of this pain, I remember thinking, *What if I'm not pregnant? Will this affect my being able to try?* Silly, right? Well I wasn't joking when I said that for the two weeks following the miscarriage, ovulation was all I could think about.

When I got to the hospital, I was immediately admitted for blood work and set up in a room to wait for my results. When the doctor finally came in, he told me that my HCG level (a hormone that shows up in pregnant women) was over one thousand. I got very excited. "I'm pregnant! That's good news, right?" I asked. It wasn't. I was informed that my levels were way too high for such an early pregnancy, and it was most likely ectopic. I was sent for an ultrasound to determine whether I would need surgery to remove the pregnancy or if a simple injection would suffice. The doctor told me that the injection would be my best bet at saving my fallopian tube. It was much better than removing the pregnancy via surgery, which would cause scarring and, in turn, put me at greater risk of having another ectopic pregnancy. After everything that had happened in the past few weeks, I was now trying to decide *how* to lose another baby! So now, aside from the fact that I was unable to keep a pregnancy, I might have the added problem of getting pregnant. Needless to say, I was furious.

The ultrasound revealed that an injection of a drug called methotrexate would be enough to cause my body to abort the pregnancy on its own, thereby avoiding the need for surgery. At least my fallopian tube would be spared! However, the blood test showed that, due to the pain I was in, my white blood cell count was high, so I would have to stay overnight and receive the injection the next day. They put me on a list to be transferred to a nearby hospital that was bigger and had an available bed for me to stay the night. What's worse, I had planned a baby shower for a good friend of mine that was to take place the next day, and I still had to finish putting together the giveaways. The nurse came in and gave me an IV to administer some morphine to help with the pain. God bless the inventor of morphine, because I was in some serious pain. She also informed me that I was not permitted to eat anything, just in case they needed to operate on me. Have you ever tried telling a woman going through trials that she can't eat? I couldn't do anything except lie there and cry. I felt as though I was trapped on a train that had been derailed. All hell was breaking loose, and I was unable to stop it.

Finally, the ambulance arrived to transfer me to

the bigger hospital, and the nurse informed me that I was to go alone. The hospital only had one small room, and my husband would not be permitted to stay the night with me. It was late when we began our journey down endless roads that weren't lit by street lights, as the ambulance wound through open fields. It was pitch black inside the ambulance and just as dark when I looked out the window. I felt as though we were driving through a black hole that closely resembled the loneliness I felt inside. I had never felt so alone and so betrayed. I had trusted God to take care of my babies, and instead He took them away. How could my loving God who had kept me and carried me all my life set out to break my heart like this?

All of a sudden, I didn't understand the God I thought I'd known. My best friend had become a stranger to me. A backstabber. A traitor. For the first time in my life, God and I were not on speaking terms. I knew that He was still there with me, but I was giving God the silent treatment. And without Him, I didn't know who to turn to in my grief. Throughout the years that followed, I sat in church, listening to the pastor speak about this God who is so strong, one who performs miracles, and with every word that came out of his mouth, I thought, *Yeah, right!* How could a God who had the power to save my babies choose not to? The problem wasn't that I'd stopped believing in God or believing that He had the power to help me. The problem was that I believed He had the power and *wasn't* helping me. If you see that someone you love is drowning, how can you stand by and watch? Nothing made sense anymore, except one thing, I needed to have a baby and I couldn't depend on God to help me do it. This became my primary goal. For the following two years it consumed me. It filled my dreams, it made my decisions, and it emptied our pockets. This child who had not even been conceived had become my new god.

Looking back now, I feel ashamed at how quickly I lost faith in God. Truly, I had been pushed to my limit. He had done the unthinkable, and I could not look past it or trust that He had everything under His control. It didn't even occur to me that I would come out of this a better person, with stronger faith, or that He had any kind of plan in all of this. Of course, I had endured other tests of my faith, but none quite as hard as this. Nothing in my life had rocked me to my core like the loss of my babies had.

Whenever I think of our journey to parenthood, the beginning is always marked by my ectopic pregnancy. Of course, it wasn't my first loss, but it marks the point in my journey where I began to question God. The exact point in time where I was no longer sure that He was on my side. This particular loss started me out on a journey through my deepest valley that, in the end, had the greatest reward.

Chapter 2

I spent the night drifting in and out of dreamless sleep. That was the first night I thought of killing myself. The morphine was strong and took away the physical pain that I was in, but I couldn't help thinking that if I could get just a little more, it would also be able to take away the pain that I felt emotionally. As I laid in that bed, I wondered what life would be like without me for those I left behind. Somehow I convinced myself that I wouldn't really be missed. My husband would find someone better who could give him tons of babies, my parents and brothers would cry, and then life would go on. I didn't want to live in this painful world any longer, and several times I contemplated praying that God would just let me die in my sleep. The only reason why I didn't pray this prayer was because I knew that He wouldn't listen. I also wondered at how quickly I had gotten to this point and realized that loss was a very difficult thing for me to deal with.

Loss had been such a constant in my life that by the time I started losing babies I was nearly driven mad. As a child, I had suffered through the breakdown of my family, the loss of a parent, a home, and many friends and family members since then. How could so much be taken away from one person? Even though I was angry with God, I was painfully aware of the fact that He was standing right there in that room with me, watching over me. I knew that He wouldn't let me die, and that I was going to live through this. Even then, in my hurt and anger, contemplating death, I knew. Although I was fuming and didn't want to call out to Him. Although I resented Him and had turned my back on Him. Although I refused to believe that He still loved me and I didn't even want to speak to Him, *still* He carried me. And I knew that somehow I would live.

Someone told me a long time ago that every day you are alive anything can go wrong, at any time. The only thing you have control over in this life, as far as trials are concerned, is your attitude. So every morning when you get up, tell yourself, "Today I will *live*, and I will live well." Now, admittedly, I wasn't living well, but I did choose to live, and that was something.

So the next day after receiving the injection to terminate my pregnancy, I left the hospital, went home, got dressed, and went to my friend's baby shower. When people hear this they often ask me why I went. Wasn't it hard for me to go to a friend's baby shower when I was in the process of losing my own baby? Yes, it was. But still I went, because I had chosen to live. And because, even then, I believed things happen in life that have the power to knock us off our feet. Not just pregnancy loss, it could be anything; hard blows that just knock the wind right out of us, and shove us into a pit of despair. But it is at the very moment that you hit the ground that you have a choice to make— *Will I stay here in this pit and rot? Or will I get up, dust myself off, and claw my way out?* As much as it hurt, I chose to get up. If I had stayed home that day, I would have gone to bed and covered my head from the world. I refused to give myself the opportunity to do so, simply because I still had hope that one day I would become a mother. I didn't know how, or when, but I knew that it would be a long road, and at the end I would be a mother.

Looking back, I can see that hope was what carried me through each of my losses. It is why I continued to live, even when I wanted to lay down and die. As long as I was alive, there was still a chance...as long as I had hope.

It was after my ectopic pregnancy that my husband and I decided to start seeing a fertility specialist. We were referred to one of the best and were put on the waiting list for an appointment with him. We didn't share this decision with many people, and those who were told had a lot to say about our decision. We were told that our decision to see a specialist showed our lack of faith in God, that as Christians we should just keep praying and trust that God will eventually heal whatever is wrong. Of course, the people making these statements had never experienced infertility themselves, nor had they ever lost a child. Even now, I still cannot understand this theory. Whenever a person feels a lump on her breast, develops a rash, or even has a really bad, long-lasting cold, no one hesitates to tell them, "Go to the doctor." So why was my decision to do just that being judged? If a woman is diagnosed with an incompetent cervix, is she any less of a Christian because she went to a doctor to find that out? If a Christian doctor diagnoses someone with a terminal illness, is that doctor any less of a Christian? I should think not. Seeing a doctor or receiving a diagnosis does not necessarily represent a lack of faith. In my case, however, it was indeed the hard hit my faith in God had taken that sent me to the clinic.

I believe that there are times when God may be telling us "Just wait, I've got this." But for me it was very difficult to just wait or to believe that God had things under control when things seemed so very out of control. At least, I reasoned, a doctor would be able to give me some answers. And I wanted answers.

I know many other women who have sought the help of specialists while they dealt with fertility issues. I think we can all agree on this one simple point—it's not for the faint of heart. The process of testing and treatment is very invasive, exhausting and, at times, painful. I just want to take the time to forewarn you if you're thinking of travelling this road. Don't get me wrong, I'm not trying to discourage you. In fact, all of the women I know who have sought the help of fertility specialists have had a successful outcome. I'm only telling you so that you can be prepared. So that you understand that the journey ahead may be a long and tiresome one. But I guarantee you that it will be worth it when you hold that baby in your arms.

Our first visit with the doctor was a short one.

He asked us a series of questions involving how long we had been trying and the nature of our miscarriages. We were booked for our first test, and we left the office feeling hopeful. We were now on our way to getting the three things we wanted the most—a diagnosis, a cure, and a baby.

The loss of my two babies still weighed heavily on my heart, but hope was in the air. My orders were to call in on the first day of my next menstrual cycle to book a blood test. I would then go in on days three, nine, twelve, and seventeen of my cycle for blood tests and ultrasounds. All of this would tell the doctors if I was ovulating regularly and at the right time in my cycle. For the first time in my life, I was excited for my period to begin. The back aches, cramps, and invasive ultrasounds would all be worth it if it brought me closer to my little one. Women, I'm sure you can all understand that when I'm not on my period I try to block it out of my mind entirely, but this time I made sure I had a tampon with me at all times as I eagerly awaited the beginning of my "journey towards fertility." Yup! That's what I called it.

However, my period did not come. Just when I was supposed to begin my "journey," I fell pregnant for the third time. This time I wasn't sure what to think. I kept hearing that as soon as I stopped trying, that's when it would happen. A thought that gave me reason to believe that maybe this time things would be different. But I also knew that I hadn't yet been tested and, therefore, had not received a diagnosis or treatment, which gave me reason to doubt. My hands were shaking as I dialed the number for the fertility clinic. They told me to come in for a blood test to confirm my pregnancy. When it was confirmed, I was instructed to come in again in two days for another blood test to check if my HCG levels were on the rise. You see, the pregnancy hormone, HCG (human chorionic gonadotropin), doubles every two days if the pregnancy is healthy. If it isn't healthy, then the HCG levels drop or fail to double every two days.

When the time came for my second blood test, I was a wreck of nerves waiting for the phone call with my results. All I could do was hope and pray that this pregnancy was viable and I wouldn't need to see the specialist after all. Finally, after an agonizing day of waiting, I got the phone call. My levels were on the rise, but they hadn't doubled. I was told to come in again in another two days but, in the meantime, to watch for spotting. As I hung up the phone, my heart felt heavy. I already knew what the next blood test would reveal. I knew that we were losing our third baby. The third blood test showed that my levels had dropped; it was labelled an early loss. I was told to purchase some extra-strength Tylenol, watch for the bleeding and cramping, and then wait for the first day of the following cycle to book my tests.

Chapter 3

This miscarriage was the most painful. I'm not sure if it was because this one was further along, but the extra-strength Tylenol felt as though it did nothing more than make me extra drowsy. The pain was excruciating, but at least it took the edge off of the emotional pain that I was drowning in. I had entered a fog of depression with this third loss. I felt like a failure, like I was cursed, and I couldn't seem to shake the feeling of guilt that I had. I felt so guilty. I knew it wasn't my fault, but I felt terrible about not being able to do the one thing that, I believed, I had a right to do as a woman. I felt guilty because my body was somehow killing my babies. I found myself constantly reliving my past sins and slip-ups, wondering if I was somehow being punished or cursed because of them. Had God *closed* my womb because of something that I had done? Something so bad that made me undeserving of children? Although I was hopeful that the tests at the clinic would give us some answers, I was ashamed that I had to go there at all. People kept asking us when we were going to start a family, and we answered, "When the time is right." But each time I uttered those words, my heart would be shouting, "*Can* I have kids?"

Just when I was about to begin testing, about to get some answers, I had to go through this, again. I was emotionally exhausted. It had never occurred to me how inconsiderate it is for people to ask a married couple when they will be starting a family. Infertility is so common that many times instead of this being a casual question, it becomes a dagger to the heart, a painful reminder that something is wrong. Not only that, but it is none of anyone's business when a couple wants to start a family. So unless someone is a close friend, they really shouldn't be asking that question. I will never forget a particular Sunday, after the third miscarriage, a fellow member of our church asked me for a ride home. I didn't really know this person or anything about her aside from her name, but I said yes, because I couldn't see the harm in helping someone out. As soon as we were alone, the questions began, one after another, without so much as a breath in between. When were Steven and I going to have kids? How many did we want? Had we talked about that yet? I sat there and drove in stunned silence, wondering how this person that I barely knew could be asking me such personal questions. I simply told her that we hadn't thought about it yet, as I pressed my foot down on the gas, increasing my speed to get her the heck out of my car.

The questions continued and, over time, I became more and more intolerable of them. A few times I actually admitted to people that we had suffered a few losses and were in the process of being tested. One woman's response was, "Oh, it's nothing! You'll probably get pregnant again tomorrow and everything will be fine." I gave her a side-eyed glare and a sharp answer. "Well, seeing as how 'probability' is not my physician of choice, I will wait to see what the doctor has to say." She hasn't spoken to me since. When I told another woman that I had suffered a miscarriage, her response was, "Oh my gosh! What does that feel like?" I gave her a scathing look, turned around, and walked away. She also hasn't spoken to me since. While the responses that these women gave were ridiculously insensitive, the truth is that most people just don't know what to say to someone who has experienced pregnancy loss or infertility. I think that people sometimes forget that a simple answer like "I'm so sorry," will suffice. And if they feel like that isn't good enough, silence is also okay.

Although I was annoyed with people's constant questions and silly responses, in some ways they helped me to find my voice. I learned that it is okay to tell someone that I don't feel comfortable being asked such personal questions, without feeling guilty for hurting their feelings. I came to understand that people who ask these questions rarely consider that maybe you are struggling with infertility or can't have kids, and aren't prepared to have an appropriate conversation if you respond with the truth. It is the same as asking a single friend when they will marry, as though there is a lineup of eligible partners and that person simply wishes to remain unattached. I have come to believe that if you are not prepared to deal with all of the information you may receive in an answer, then you have no business asking the question. I have also come to believe that "How are you?" and "fine" are the new hellos of the twenty-first century. This insignificant verbal exchange gives us the illusion that we have become more intimate in our greetings, while the truth is that we have sunk deeper into the abyss of loneliness and untruth. In the two and a half years that we went through five pregnancy losses and a myriad of tests, I must have been asked how I was hundreds of times, and each time I responded with "Fine," when I was anything but.

As we began our testing, we were painfully aware that the process could take over a year, and in the meantime, we settled into the waiting game. I will always remember this period as the *eye of the storm*. A restless calm settled over our marriage as we carried on with our lives, wondering how many more tests we would have to endure before we reached an answer, and what that answer would be when it finally came. Some days it was as though things were normal. We smiled and laughed together and even spoke of a future with our children, planning fun trips and activities for when they get older. During these times, neither of us voiced out loud the question that we were both wondering—*Will we have these children that we were planning for?* We had no answer to that question, and so we continued to plan, in the hopes that the answer was yes.

When we were finally able to complete the first

series of blood tests and ultrasounds, it was confirmed that I was ovulating regularly and on time, and I was given a referral for another test with a name that I still cannot pronounce. That test was to show if one of my fallopian tubes was blocked. Again, everything looked normal, and I was moved on to my next test. I went through each procedure hoping that it would produce an answer, something that was wrong that could be fixed. But nothing was ever wrong. The specialist recommended that I take a prescription that would make me ovulate more than once per cycle, giving me a greater chance of achieving conception. He also had me take an injection at ovulation that would ensure that the eggs were released, plus some capsules that I had to insert, you know where, which would help the embryo to grow if we conceived. And all the while, the doctor told us, "Don't worry, we'll keep trying." I know that may seem pretty easy with all the sex we were having, but trust me, it wasn't.

Sex was no longer sex. Sex became 'trying.' Every time we had sex, it was with a purpose, and all of our efforts went towards making sure my husband 'made his contribution.' But no one ever told us how hard it would be to perform under stress, and that sometimes we would miss the mark. Sometimes we missed ovulation altogether because he was too stressed to 'complete the mission.' He knew that if he didn't finish I would have to go through more tests, more invasive procedures. But it was just too much, and sex was no longer fun.

Chapter 4

While I travelled the journey through the eye of the storm, enduring several more invasive tests, my war with God raged on. I became ashamed to speak to people about my Christianity, especially if they knew about our pregnancy losses. After all, I told myself, this was hardly an advertisement for Christianity, and I really didn't know if I could explain how God was going to fix everything when it didn't look like He was fixing anything. I refrained from admitting my beliefs, because I didn't know how I would answer if I was asked how this trial was affecting my faith. I couldn't admit that my faith in God had been hit hard. I couldn't explain how my babies kept dying while other babies, whose mothers seemed less deserving, stayed alive. We read newspaper articles about children being abused by parents, and thought, *How did these people get pregnant?* We heard stories about people who already had four children when they became pregnant with twins, *accidentally*. And we knew someone who was on birth control, not even trying to get pregnant, and did. I will never forget the day I got that news; I was quiet the entire drive home. Anyone who knows me will have trouble believing this, but it's true. Dead silence. When we got home, I calmly got out of the car, took off my shoes and placed them neatly on the shoe rack (another sign that I had truly lost it), walked slowly up the stairs, went into the guest room, got down on my knees beside the bed, folded my hands, closed my eyes, and shouted, "Seriously?" That was the entire prayer. That one word pretty much summed up how I felt. The truth was that I still loved God tremendously, but I could no longer trust Him. I didn't understand Him, but I desperately needed Him. A fact that made me even angrier.

Each test revealed nothing wrong, yet I had already lost three babies. So, clearly, there was something wrong, but the doctors couldn't figure out what it was. Our prayers didn't seem to be helping, and through all of the testing and trying, I still lost another baby. Miscarriage number four. Or five. We also had one 'barely there' pregnancy with a very faint positive that turned into a negative two days later.

That particular loss was the big one. The straw that broke the camel's back. The catalyst that threw me over the edge of sanity and into a maddened frenzy to procreate. I also spent hours online researching adoption. The different types, waiting periods, costs, financial aid, and so forth. But I was determined to try one more time. Just once more. And if that didn't work, then we were adopting. I was sick and tired of waiting, and

I was going to make this happen. I continued to go to the clinic for almost daily ultrasounds and blood tests so that they could tell us the optimal time to try. Again. But then we got word that the specialist wanted to meet with us to review our file. I was already upset over the lack of progress and frustrated because I knew that the staff at the clinic were doing all they could to help us meet our goal, so I wondered what new information the doctor could possibly have for us. I sat in the office and listened while he conveyed his sympathy over our recent loss, told us of his plans to try IVF, and asked if we were comfortable with the possibility of twins. He also listed the series of tests that we had already completed, but something was wrong. He mentioned a blood test. A complete analytical blood evaluation, he said. But I had never received such a test since visiting the clinic. When I told him so, he replied, "But you must have, it was the first test I recommended for you." I told him again that I didn't have the test done and asked him if the test was really necessary. That's when he dropped the bomb. "This was the first test you were supposed to take. It will show me your hormone levels and several other pieces of information, which could reveal any number of causes for your losses."

I sat silently as the information settled like a haze in the room. "So...this one test could have saved me from having to do all of the other tests, including the minor surgery that also revealed nothing?

"Um..." he quietly responded, "well, yes."

"And if something does show up, we could have possibly prevented the past two losses?"

He silently nodded. "I am so sorry, Judine," he said, "you will definitely receive a letter of apology from the clinic, and I will put you on the waitlist for the test, right now."

That's when I snapped. In fact, I'm pretty sure we both actually *heard* the snap, as I calmly leaned over the desk, looked him dead in the eyes and said, "I do not want your letter of apology because, unless it is coming laced with sperm, it will not give me a baby. And you are now recommending IVF. Why? So we can pay thousands of dollars to lose two babies at a time? No. What I want is for you to fix this mistake. Now. I am not leaving this clinic until I receive that blood test that I should have received a year and a half ago, when I first came here. And do not bother to tell me that there is a waitlist and that there are other women ahead of me, because if this blood test reveals something, then you and your staff have already cost me two babies, and unless those women out there can say the same, then I am not leaving here without taking the test." I leaned back in my chair and folded my arms as he picked up the phone and told the receptionist that he was sending me into the waiting room for a complete analytical blood test and that I was to go in next before any other patient.

He told me that he would call me with the results, and I politely thanked him and went in for my test. I was sure that this had to be it. The missing link that would finally give us an answer. But after ten vials of blood, everything came back normal and, again, we were left feeling dumbfounded. Needless to say I was absolutely humiliated after I so rudely demanded to have the test taken, only to have it come back without answers. We were instructed to go through one more cycle of ovulation induction and, if it was unsuccessful, we would come in for another evaluation.

When the clinic finally called and told us it was time to try again for that night and the following two days, I was determined to be successful this time. It was Friday, which meant we had the whole weekend. Plus, we were informed that two eggs had matured, which meant we had a doubled chance at getting pregnant and a possibility of twins! We knew that if we failed, then we would be left with IVF, and the financial burden that came with it. This thought added so much extra pressure that my already stressed out husband had a hard time remaining 'focused.' We tried several times on the Friday night, because we were convinced that he needed to finish at least once a day for that entire weekend in order to give us the best chance at conceiving. But as much as we tried, things proved to be more and more difficult each time. It was hours before he was able to finish. And even though we did it, as I laid with my hips propped up on some pillows—so gravity could help the sperm travel in the right direction—I cried. It was just too stressful. I was exhausted, physically, mentally, and emotionally. And it was only Friday.

The next day we rested for the morning, cancelled our evening plans, and got to work again around noon. I call it *work* because that's exactly what it felt like. Neither of us was excited about the prospect of an evening filled with sex, because we knew that we had a mission to accomplish and that it would be a hard one. I tried to put on a brave face with some lingerie, romantic music, and good humour, but after the first three tries, I was in tears. I left the room and sat by myself and cried. I knew that my husband was in the next room fighting his own emotional battle, feeling guilty about not being able to do his part, but it became harder to get aroused with each failed attempt. After some time apart, he came to find me. We sat together, sharing how we felt about this whole process. The vote was unanimous, we were done trying. This weekend would be the last time. We both agreed that we would continue trying that night and the next day, and then try IVF. He told me that he felt like he was failing me because he couldn't do his part. He knew how much I was depending on him, but the stress of the past year and a half had taken its toll emotionally, and it was too hard for him to forget it long enough to get through this weekend. I told him that my body was exhausted from all of the tests and treatments and that I felt like a failure as a woman, because I couldn't do what a woman should be able to do. Although it sounded ridiculous, I was angry at my body for failing me, for attacking my babies, and for refusing to operate properly. I was angry at us for not being able to do something that was once so easy for us. It used to be fun! Before we started 'trying,' sex and baby-making were one and the same, but somehow they had become two separate things, and the latter was all we seemed to do anymore. It was not fun.

After unloading our heavy hearts, we got up and went back in together, sad but willing. We tried and tried for a few more hours, unsuccessfully, before I was in tears, again. This time I got angry. I cried and yelled. At God. At life. At Steven. I was doing most of the work. Going through every invasive test and procedure; every single staff member at the clinic had had a one-on-one with my vagina! The only job he had was to have successful sex. Was that so hard? I told him that he was failing me. I begged him to come through for me. To please, please come through for me, because I had done all that I could, given all that my body could handle, and I needed this war to be over. I needed him to do this for me. To get himself together and focus! I even suggested going online to find some erotic story or video to help him. I was *that* desperate.

Looking back, I truly believe that I lost my mind that night. For a few brief hours, I lost my mind. Almost two years, four losses, innumerable, invasive, sometimes painful, tests had become too heavy a burden to bear, and I had finally crumbled under the weight of it all. I screamed and yelled, until I was spent and collapsed into a heap of tears on the floor, while Steven sat with his head in his hands. Then after hours of intense silence, he suggested we try again. We had no choice. After two more tries, he did it. To this day I have no idea how my husband got himself to finish that night. I know that a crying, screaming, panicking, angry woman can never be sexy. But, somehow, he did it.

Chapter 5

I woke up the next morning with a clear head, and it was then that I realized how badly I had behaved. It was then that I realized I had actually lost it. I replayed the whole episode from the night before and I was baffled at how completely crazy I had become. I knew that I was done. IVF would have to wait. I was done. My body was done. I had lost all of my faith in God and, in doing so, I had lost myself. It never occurred to me how much a part of me God was, until I lost him. You see, when something is such a big part of you and you lose it, you lose yourself as well. I felt defeated and weak and lost. I apologized to my husband for the way I behaved. He told me that he understood that I was just exhausted and angry, and he forgave me. We tried again, successfully, that day without the drama, romance, or pleasure. It was strictly business, as we did what we agreed to do and spent the rest of the day in silence.

We waited, hopefully, to see if we were pregnant. Maybe all of the fighting and struggling would be worth it if we finally had a baby. We were scared when we found out we were indeed pregnant, but now the focus was on keeping it, when we still didn't know what was wrong. After completing my second blood test at the clinic to see if the pregnancy was viable, I went to work, keeping my phone in my pocket all day as I waited for the phone call. When they did call, the news wasn't good. An early loss.

As I walked back to class I ran into a parent, a father whose wife had just given birth to their third child that morning. I pasted on a fake smile and quickly congratulated him on the birth of his daughter. A sentiment to which he replied, "Yeah, but too bad she didn't come on the weekend. I really didn't want to have to take a day off work for this." I didn't even respond to him. I couldn't. I silently turned around and returned to the washroom where I collapsed on the floor and cried. I knew that I didn't have the strength emotionally to go through with IVF, and we had lost our last chance. It was over. When I returned to the classroom, my co-teacher knew immediately what had happened. She left the class and came back a few minutes later with another teacher. They gathered my stuff, placed them in my arms and told me to go home and rest. I left the school, got in my car, and drove home. When I got home, I went straight up to my room, took more than the recommended amount of sleeping pills and curled up in bed beside my cat, closed my eyes, and slept.

Over the next few weeks, I found it harder and harder to sleep, so I began taking various pills to help me. Two Gravol, four Tylenol, anything that would make me drowsy enough to sleep. If no pills were found, I drank enough to knock me out. I had a water bottle filled with alcohol hidden under the sink in the bathroom, so I could access it easily if I couldn't fall asleep. My only other option was to lie awake all night thinking about my miscarriages, my disappointing reproductive system, and my lost faith in God. I was drowning, and I didn't care. Even as I'm writing this, I am ashamed and terrified. I know that one day people will read my book and they're going to know everything. They're going to know how bad things got and how poorly I dealt with them. Some of these people know me. *Will they look at me differently? Will they think I'm weak?*

I tried talking to some of my Christian friends, but the answers were all the same—just keep praying! Keep believing. I honestly believe that they say these things because they really have no idea what else to say to a woman in my predicament. But I felt all prayed out and I had no hope left in my heart. So what came next? I had no idea. Why couldn't I have a real conversation with other Christians about my struggle? Sometimes Christians use Christ as a smokescreen; we tell each other to pray, because we don't want to get deep and share what we really think. We don't want to discuss unanswered prayers, because we don't actually know why these prayers have gone unanswered. What do we say after we join together in prayer, believing God will answer, and see no results? We pray expecting God to hear and deliver, but could it be possible that there is another answer? Could it be that the answer is no? Or not yet?

I have to say that out of all of the periods in my

life, I learned the most about myself during this one. The one thing that hit me hard was something I like to call *spiritual arrogance*. You see, I believed that, as a Christian, I had a right to have all of my prayers answered. It didn't matter whether I truly needed or was ready to handle what I was asking for. I was a Bible-thumping Christian, and I deserved answered prayers. Every. Single. Time. I had always been taught that asking God for something was like rubbing a magic lamp and having my wishes granted by some magical genie. That if I declared and decreed then I would have what I wanted. Isn't this what most pastors preach nowadays? The name-it-claim-it Christians who say if you're not claiming it then *you* are the problem. Maybe you're not believing hard enough. Maybe you just have to hold on a little bit longer. Perhaps you've done something wrong that is stopping your blessing; a cursed item in the camp, maybe? Have you paid your tithes? Have you pledged enough to the church building fund? Maybe some more money would get you to your blessing. Well, here's an idea that most Christians today aren't familiar with. No. Not yet. Simple words that every parent must at some point tell their children.

Now, I believe God to be my Father, and I don't think anyone can accuse God of having poor parenting skills. So what good parent just gives their child everything they ask for? I couldn't help but wonder, *Was God leading me through this valley?* If I really wanted to stick to the popular belief that my steps are "ordered by God," then I had to know that, despite how things looked, I was just where I was supposed to be. There was some character to gain, new skills to be acquired, and lessons to be learned. And I had to learn them on my own.

All of the questions that I had always been taught not to ask, I now felt compelled to ask. Why do some prayer requests go unanswered? Does God *always* give us what we are asking for? Honestly, I don't think so. When I gave myself permission to question God, I began to feel the weight on my shoulders lift off. Because He answered me. All of a sudden I saw God in a different light. I saw Him as a parent, a father. I realized that He had heard me when I asked Him for what I really wanted, and He was answering. It was I who wasn't listening. He was saying, "Not yet." He was trying to get me to take my hands off of the situation and just leave it with Him to bless me in His own time. I knew that the doctor would never be able to help me, God wanted it to be Him, and He would have it no other way. Now don't get me wrong. I'm not saying that Christians aren't supposed to seek the help of doctors in situations like this. What I am saying is that this was what God required of me. I know many people who have dealt with infertility and pregnancy loss. For some, it was something that they had to wait on God for; for others, they went to the doctor and received help. For others, they chose to adopt. The point is you need to ask God which path He wants you to take. Each path will come with its own set of hardships, but the successful path will be the one that God has for you.

This revelation brings to mind the story of Abraham and Sarah. God told Sarah that she would conceive and have a son, but after waiting and waiting, it seemed as though God had forgotten about her. Sound familiar? Due to her loss of faith, she had her husband sleep with her handmaiden to produce the child that they were still waiting for. We all know what happened. Her handmaiden gave birth to a son, but soon after God kept His word, and Sarah did indeed get pregnant. Ishmael was a son born out of impatience and a lack of faith. Isaac was the one God promised He would send. This is a story that speaks volumes to women struggling with infertility and wondering which path to take. I considered adoption when we failed to conceive, because I no longer believed that God would answer our prayers and help me carry a baby. If we had adopted, that child would have been our Ishmael. A child brought into our home because of our lack of faith in God. Adoption isn't bad, but it wasn't what God wanted for us. I know another couple who also tried for years to have a baby. They considered adoption, but the woman stubbornly refused, wanting badly to carry a child of her own. However, after some time, she was able to open her heart to the realization that God was calling her to adopt. This was not an easy choice, because choosing to adopt meant admitting that she could not bear children naturally, something that she had not been ready to admit up until then. When she finally chose to allow God to lead them into parenthood in His own way, they began the long and stressful process that comes with adoption, and after a lengthy wait they were chosen by a birth mother. The night that they finally got the call to come meet their son was a very emotional one. They rushed to the hospital and were met by a nurse who brought them into a room where their new son was waiting. As soon as the new mother saw her baby, she knew, this was her 'Isaac.' This was the baby that God had for them. If you are struggling with the decision of whether to adopt or to hold out, pray and ask God to reveal His perfect will for you. Don't settle for Ishmael when God has Isaac waiting for you.

Every woman dealing with infertility will have a different story. A different ending. After all I have been through, I now believe that stuff just happens. Sounds simple, huh? Well it is. It is true that, regardless of your faith, when the sun shines, it shines on the good and the bad. Likewise, when the rain falls, it falls on the bad and the good. I know that this is not the answer you are looking for; it certainly doesn't explain why this is happening to you. Quite frankly, this answer sucks. But this is the plain and simple truth. What you are going through could be the single worst experience in your life and, to make it worse, there seems to be absolutely nothing you can do about it. The only thing that you have control over is your attitude and, I'm sure you already know, it is likely hard to have a good attitude about anything right now. I believe that while the life experiences we have may not be pleasant, it is up to us to handle them with grace. It is our attitude alone that can determine whether this storm is temporary or if it will become a permanent disaster in our lives. I have learned that it is okay to grieve. I mean really grieve. It is okay to question your beliefs and to wonder why. After all, it is easier to believe in a thing when you have found it for yourself as opposed to having witnessed another finding it.

So ask your questions and then give time for the answers. Some you will get right away, some you will stumble across at some point in your life, while others you will have to deliberately seek out. But understand that there are some answers that you will never get. You may never know the answer to your biggest and most pressing question at this time. You may never know why. I know that this is a hard pill to swallow. Even now, after all this time, I still often look back and wonder why this all happened. Why to me? And even now, after all this time, I still have no answer and, most likely, I never will. Even if there is a medical reason that caused your loss or infertility, you will still find that you are asking why. I am not saying this to discourage you; I am only telling you the truth. I know it is hard to face the reality of this situation, but you must try to look forward. Because the truth is, life does go on. Time passes, and things *do* get better. For some of you, the next pregnancy will be successful. Some of you may endure more pain before your successful pregnancy. Some of you may be diagnosed with something that can be fixed and then walk the road towards better days. While others may be diagnosed with infertility. You may choose to adopt—and I truly hope you do—or you may give up hope of ever becoming a parent. I cannot tell you what the future holds, but I can tell you that there is a path that is right for you.

After our sixth loss, we were called in for another follow-up with our fertility specialist. I was diagnosed with unexplained infertility. After all this time and all of the invasive tests, they didn't know what was wrong. And to top it all off, we were no longer considered candidates for IVF, a procedure designed to help women who are unable to get pregnant naturally, which was something I had no trouble doing. Since they couldn't discover why I kept losing my babies, they didn't think that IVF would help, as it isn't a procedure that can prevent miscarriage. It was becoming increasingly clear that God was telling us to wait on *Him*.

Maybe God is also telling you to wait on Him. Or maybe a doctor will help to diagnose a problem and treat it. Maybe God has another baby out there for you. A baby that you will not carry in your womb, but a baby that you will love as if you had. I can tell you this, somehow, someway, someday you are going to be a mother. Listen to His voice and find the path that is right for *you*. Don't give up on God!

Chapter 6

That summer I returned to church. Of course, I had attended services throughout my struggle, but mentally I was an inactive participant in worship and the Word. This first Sunday back, as worship began, I sat in my seat and bowed my head to pray. As the congregation sang and clapped around me, I sat and emptied myself out before God. I asked God to show me how to keep Him. Because if I didn't, I would lose myself completely, and then what kind of person would I be? What kind of parent would I be? How can a broken person raise a healthy child? I couldn't. Not like this. I knew then that I could lose ten more babies, but I couldn't lose God. I begged God to show me how to have faith in Him. To show me how to hold on to Him when the storm gets really bad and the skies go pitch black. I knew He loved me, and I *needed* to love Him back. I *needed* to love Him, again. And, just like that, it happened. I was in His arms, again. Still without a baby, but safe, unharmed, loved, protected, and, once again, hopeful.

From that day, I devoted my time to everything other than trying to conceive. I attended rehearsals for a play that I had been cast in, spent time with my family, and began writing this book. I wanted other women to know that they were not alone in their struggle, and although my story wasn't yet complete, I knew that the storm had passed. I wanted other women to find peace in their storm as well. I still watched mothers with their kids in the store, and felt a little jealous when I saw a pregnant woman walk by, but thankfully, I was able to sleep without taking any pills, and I awoke every morning feeling rested. But the best part was that sex was fun! My husband and I fell in love again and spent a lot of quality time together, healing and laughing. We decided to wait for at least six months before even talking about a baby, and what a relief!

Summer came, and with it a busy schedule packed with rehearsal after rehearsal for the play that I had been cast in. I had always loved the stage, and being able to connect with it once again revived my weathered spirit and filled me with joy. The other cast members were fun, energetic, and *real*. Among them I found a place to be free. Surrounded by kindred spirits, each with a story of their own, I no longer felt isolated. Although our struggles were quite different, we saw in each other the same willingness to fight whatever demons were plaguing us, and lend one another the strength to overcome our challenges. And boy, did we have fun.

Each rehearsal felt like a vacation from the past two years, and I enjoyed myself immensely. When we got word that we were being asked to bring the play over to the UK, I was beyond excited. I hoped and prayed (yes, I was praying again) that I would be chosen to go, and I was! I began planning for my trip, booked the time off work, and attended the extra scheduled rehearsals for the cast that was going overseas. Everything was going smoothly. But leave it to God to spice things up just when the meal's gone bland.

On Sunday, August 19, 2013, my husband and I attended church together. We weren't very happy to be there this particular Sunday, because our god-daughter was being Christened in Connecticut, but we were unable to make the trip there for the service, so we found ourselves at home in our own church. That Sunday, our pastor decided to read the testimony of another church member who had struggled to conceive in the past. We listened to him tell of how she had come to him for prayer, and shortly afterwards she conceived and gave birth to twins. After reading this testimony, he declared that he wanted to pray for anyone in the congregation who was having trouble starting a family. He wanted us all to come up to the front and stand together while he prayed for us. As couple after couple passed us on their way to the front, we remained firmly planted in our seats. We had prayed so many times in the past. In fact, our pastor had already prayed with us in the beginning of our struggle. But through the years, whenever he would check up on us, we still had no testimony to tell. So we sat there, refusing to move, and all the while I heard a gentle voice inside saying, "Try God one more time."

"But we did try God! We tried Him FIRST!" I argued.

And again I heard it, "Try God one more time."

So I reached over and took Steven's hand. We got up and made our way to the front, just as our pastor began his prayer. As we made our way back to our seats afterwards, for the first time since this whole ordeal had begun, I felt certain that God was going to answer our prayers. I'm not sure exactly what changed in my heart, but I felt... *different*. I felt at peace. I didn't know when our baby would arrive, but I knew that it would.

On September 2, 2013, two weeks later, I found out that I was pregnant for the seventh time. My period was a week overdue, but I was terrified to take a home pregnancy test. I figured, *Why not wait it out? Then if I have another miscarriage, technically I won't really know that it's a miscarriage; it will just be a late period.* I went through a mental checklist of symptoms daily. Morning sickness, nope. Dizziness, nope. Cravings, nope. Sore breasts...maybe. *See? Not nearly enough symptoms to be a pregnancy.* What a relief! But deep down I didn't feel so relieved, because maybe, just maybe. So finally I went out and reluctantly bought a home pregnancy test. Upon my return home, I abandoned the test and busied myself doing chores around the house. I was a nervous wreck. After some time, I gave in. After all, I couldn't hold my pee a minute longer. After peeing on the stick, I placed the test on the counter as far as I could reach. I didn't want to be tempted to look before the three minutes were up. I got up, took a shower, got dressed, and paced the floors. I didn't want to look!

So, once again, I went through my mental checklist of symptoms, reminded myself that my period had been late before. *But what if those weren't late periods?* I wondered. *What if they were miscarriages that I just didn't know about? But sometimes your period could just be late, right? Maybe I should look it up online. See? It says right here, sometimes your period could just be late!* Now I was convinced it was just a late period. I was almost confident that the test was negative. I finally caved and went to toss the certainly negative test. But as I entered the bathroom, I froze in my steps. Because it wasn't negative. It was positive.

I snatched the test off of the counter and brought it close to my face, so I could see it better. Instantly, the bathroom filled with a loud voice praying, declaring that there was life in my womb. Praising God and asking Him to help this baby to live. The voice was so loud and spoke with such authority that I was surprised to find that the voice was my own. It was so instantaneous, so powerful. I had never prayed like that before. There were no tears or begging God to please, please spare this life. I remembered my pastor's prayer, the voice of God urging us to try Him just once more, and I couldn't help but wonder, was this it? Was this the baby we had been praying for all along? Had my turn actually come?

Now, I know what you're thinking. You think that we were overjoyed, that we were confident, and nine months later, presto, baby. Well, I hate to burst your bubble, but if you've ever lost a baby, then you know that miscarriage robs you not just of a child, but of the innocence of a first pregnancy. I no longer had the ability to just trust that all would be well and the baby would come. It is unfortunate, but once you learn how quickly and easily something can be taken away, you never forget. I refused to go to the doctor right away. I just couldn't bear to hear the words "early loss," "no heartbeat," or "low HCG levels." So I put off going. My husband, of course, was not comfortable with this decision, so after weeks of persuasion, I called and made an appointment. At eight weeks pregnant, I finally decided to seek prenatal care.

When my doctor learned how far along I was, she was appalled. Given my history, she asked why I would wait so long to seek medical attention. She scheduled an ultrasound right away, and quickly squashed any hope I had of travelling overseas to do the play. I was crushed. I just didn't want to cancel a trip that I was so excited about for a pregnancy that may end just like all the others. Although Steven tried to assure me that God was answering our prayers, the scars of the past began to feel like fresh wounds, bringing back bad memories and old fears. Ironically, my first ultrasound was booked for the same day that the cast was leaving for the UK, a coincidence that only heightened my anxiety. *What if the ultrasound revealed nothing, just as the cast was leaving without me? What if I gave up this opportunity for no reason?* True, there had been no spotting, but there had also been no morning sickness or any of the other typical signs of pregnancy, a fact that led me to believe that all was not well. The morning before the ultrasound, I was a living disaster. Tears. Everywhere. My daily mental checklist of symptoms had not revealed nearly enough to convince me that I would hear good news.

I left work early and met my husband at the clinic for the ultrasound. By this time, I had exhausted myself with worry and could do nothing more than wait. When my name was called, I went in, undressed, and laid on the table. The ultrasound technician quietly moved the probe over my tummy as I waited anxiously for the news. She was so quiet, and her face gave no indication of whether the news was good or bad. Then she moved her hand away, looked at me with a blank expression, and said, "Okay, now go empty your bladder." I was astonished! That was it?

"But what about the baby?" I asked.

"Oh yes, everything is fine. The baby is fine," she muttered. I bolted upright and pushed my head in between her and the computer screen. I couldn't believe my eyes. There, in the middle of the screen, was a tiny little blob that looked almost like a strawberry. My baby was alive!

"That's it?" I asked.

"Yes," she said, "that's the baby."

I burst into tears and started sobbing like a maniac in front of a complete stranger, who was now looking at me like I had grown an extra head. I was so embarrassed. I frantically tried to compose myself while informing her of my past miscarriages and telling her just how much it meant to me to finally see a baby on the screen. Her face softened and she gently told me to lie back down. "I'll get you a good picture to take home."

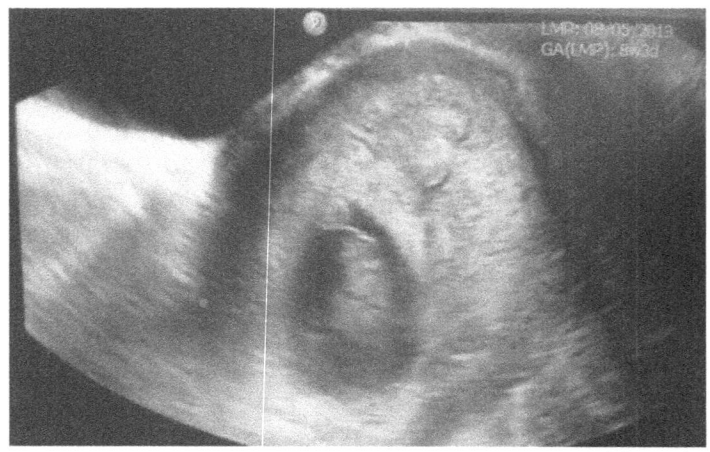

at 8 weeks

After the ultrasound, I came back out into the waiting room where my husband was, no doubt, on pins and needles. I quietly held out the picture given to me by the technician. "This is our baby."

Again, I know you're probably thinking that things went well from here on out. But you're wrong. I hate to admit it, but that wasn't the final crisis of faith during my pregnancy. You see, while most women dread the constant nausea that comes with pregnancy, my lack of morning sickness gave me no comfort. I desperately craved the daily confirmation that I was still pregnant. In fact, looking back, my pregnancy was the kind that every woman dreams about. No morning sickness, no dizziness, no uncomfortable aches and pains. And to top it all off, after having the baby I was four pounds *lighter* than before I got pregnant. That's right, I lost weight during the pregnancy, despite the fact that I gave in to every craving I had—salt and vinegar chips, poutine, sweet poutine, ginger ale, and Swiss Chalet. But all of this good fortune gave me reason to question whether all was right with the world.

By twelve weeks pregnant, Steven and I were making plans to go the annual Baby Time Show. I should have been ecstatic but, once again, I had allowed my past experiences to resurrect new fears. I spent the night before the expo in tears, asking myself, *What if we go and buy things for a baby that no longer exists?* I am crying as I write this. I can still taste the fear that I felt that night. Thank God for His patience! Even after He had answered my prayers, my faith in Him was still weak. I was terrified of being let down, again. Terrified of falling in love with a baby I may never get to hold. But God is so merciful. As we walked into the expo the next day, we were immediately greeted by a woman advertising 3D ultrasounds. Regular price $175, but only $75 for the guests at the Baby Time Show. I guess God knew that in order for me to enjoy myself and finally trust that my baby would live, I needed to see it with my own two eyes. As we waited for our turn, we browsed through the shops that were all around and saw a few things that we wanted to purchase. I convinced Steven to hold off until after the ultrasound. We hadn't seen the baby since eight and a half weeks, anything could have happened. My husband looked at me like I was crazy. "You haven't had any spotting so what would make you think that anything is wrong? You need to relax!" he encouraged.

As we made our way back for our ultrasound, I tried to convince myself that Steven was right.

After all, there really wasn't any evidence to prove that our baby was in danger. As the technician began to slide the probe over my tummy, I said a quiet prayer and turned my head to look at the screen. Within seconds, the image popped up. What an active little thing! Tears ran down my face as I watched my little peanut kick and turn. I had never seen anything so magical before.

"We might be able to tell the sex of the baby. Are you interested in knowing?" asked the technician.

We both replied with a frantic "Yes!"

She gently moved the probe to one side and pressed in. "It looks like a boy!"

That will always remain one of the most precious and memorable moments of my life. We left the ultrasound booth and headed back over to the shops, where we bought two blankets and some baby spoons for our son.

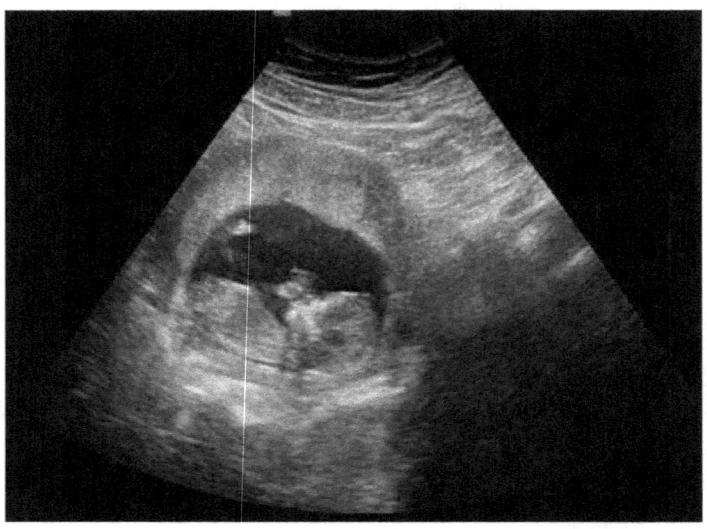

at 12 weeks

Chapter 7

As we drove home later on that day, it finally became real—I was having a baby. I was going to be a mom. This was really happening! I finally began to relax into my pregnancy and plan for my baby. From that day on, I was in military mode. I began to make list after list of what we needed to get, what we needed to do, and what we needed to know. I included timelines and deadlines for all of our preparations and, as I write about it now, I thank God that my husband didn't leave me!

I'm not sure how he put up with my constant plans and preparations, but he handled it like a pro. I sure do love him. And, thankfully, this was the final crisis of faith in my pregnancy. I actually began to enjoy my pregnancy. While many mothers hate the thought of getting bigger, I adored my growing belly. I wore clothes to accentuate its roundness. I couldn't stop touching it. My baby was in there. My sweet Alexander.

The first time I felt my Alex kick was amazing.

Every day after that I would spend time poking and prodding my bump, hoping to feel another little nudge. It was then that it became clear that my son sleeps like his father. Once the eyes close, any and all surroundings disappear. At my twenty-week ultrasound, I was informed that they would be measuring all of the baby's parts, including his head. They also wanted to have a look at his facial features to ensure that he was developing well. However, in order to measure his head and look at his face he would have to move. His head was buried deep in my pelvis, and they needed him to turn in order to complete the ultrasound. The nurse sent me to have a walk and to drink something sweet. "This usually gets baby moving," she said.

But no amount of sugar or cardio could get him up. We had to reschedule the appointment. Twice. Alex became known at the clinic as 'the baby who sleeps,' and whenever we went in the receptionist would ask, "Is he awake today?" Everyone at the clinic knew that once Alex was asleep, he was asleep. And he also did not like ultrasounds. He disliked anything that pressed up against my belly.

We went to a specialist who was supposed to look into his heart to ensure that it was developing well. Because of my history, the doctors wanted to make sure that everything was normal. After the ultrasound, the doctor needed to listen to his heartbeat for one whole minute and count the beats. This part took much longer than just a minute. Every time the doctor pressed the probe to my tummy, Alex would kick it off. He kicked so hard that we would hear a loud "BAM" in the mic, and the probe would jump. So, for several minutes, all we heard was the whoosh, whoosh, whoosh of his heartbeat, then BAM! Whoosh, whoosh, whoosh, BAM! Even though he was still inside of me, he already had quite a personality.

There were days when I thought that the fear that had ruled my life for so long had finally left me. Days when I would be bursting with joy. But the thing about loss is that it teaches you not to get comfortable. It teaches you that anything can be taken away, just like that. So although things were going well in my pregnancy, I still found myself plagued with fear that something would go wrong. If a period of time passed without any movement from down below, I'd spend endless hours poking my tummy, just to feel one kick. I would imagine giving birth to a dead baby or that something would be wrong with him when he was born. One thing I now know for sure is that fear is a jerk. If fear were a person, I'd punch him in the face! By the end of my pregnancy, around thirty weeks, I became so sick and tired of living in fear. I wanted to live confidently. I wanted to *know* that my baby would be born healthy, strong, and alive.

I had prayed every day for my baby up to this point, and then I found myself praying less for the baby and more for myself. I prayed for God to help me to believe in Him. I prayed that He would grant me courage to face each day with confidence. I prayed for peace of mind and thanked God every morning and every night that my Alex was still alive.

At thirty-seven weeks and one day, I went into labour. On April 23, 2014 at 3:47 a.m. my water broke. I had always seen this happen in the movies—the woman is standing there and suddenly water begins flowing out of her like Niagara Falls. This is how I thought it would be, until I got older and was told otherwise. All of my friends and colleagues whose water had broken had informed me that when it happens it's nothing more than a mere trickle. One parent told me that she thought she was peeing herself, because the flow wasn't very heavy. Well, I can now verify that it *can* be the way you see it in the movies. When my water broke, it was no trickle. It was the movie kind of Niagara Falls flow that I had imagined as a child. I was lying in bed when I felt a sudden pop 'down there' and suddenly I was drowning in bed. I quickly woke up my husband and told him it was time to go. We frantically ran around the room getting dressed and grabbing our hospital bags, while I left a trail of water in my path. Several sanitary napkins were no match for the major flow. I grabbed a thick towel from our linen closet, folded it up, placed it on the passenger seat, and hopped in as my husband took off for the hospital. On the way there, I felt a second pop and the major flow became a major gush. I couldn't believe how anyone could mistake this for pee. When we arrived at the hospital, we made our way to Labour and Delivery, where I informed the nurse that my water had broken. I stood before the desk, soaked, with water continuing to gush out of me, forming a puddle on the ground around my feet. I guess the nurse didn't see all of this, because she replied, "I have to swab you to make sure that your waters have actually broken."

I looked at her, then down at the growing puddle about my feet. "Seriously?" I asked. "I can assure you I don't pee like this."

But still she insisted, so we followed her to the assessment room where we waited for a nurse to come and verify that I wasn't peeing. After an hour, she finally arrived, collected her sample and proudly informed me that my water had broken and I was in labour. I was not amused. Why do professionals need a swab to tell them what plain old fashion eyesight could tell them in less time?

Once it was confirmed that I was in labour, I was moved into our labour and delivery room. I know you've probably heard a thousand horror stories of what goes on during labour, but I have no such story to tell. Because my water broke before my contractions started, I had the pleasure of receiving an early epidural and not feeling any of them. Once it was time to push I still couldn't feel anything, and I pushed the baby out within eleven minutes. The only thing I can say was that my labour process was long. Eighteen hours of waiting, and I was starving! I had eaten an early dinner the evening before, around 3:30 p.m., so that I wouldn't have to suffer with the indigestion that plagued me every night. My water broke twelve hours later and another twelve hours after that, at 3:30 p.m., I was still only dilated three centimetres. Twenty-four hours without a single bite. By 5:00 p.m., the doctor on shift recommended a C-section because I wasn't progressing at all. He also told me that I had to stop drinking water. I mean, by this point I was so hungry that every sip of water tasted like fried chicken. However, as that doctor's shift ended at 5:00 p.m. and another doctor started his, things quickly changed.

The new doctor came in, assessed me, increased

my Pitocin and said, "No C-section for you. This baby's going to come on his own." And he was right. By 10:50 p.m. I was ready to push. Within minutes, a nurse came in to remove my epidural and sent me into an outright panic. I begged her not to remove it, as I was terrified to push without it. The horror stories I had heard of women tearing badly had terrified me to my very soul, and I didn't want to feel a thing while I was pushing. The nurse calmly informed me that the doctor didn't like to have women push with the epidural, because if we couldn't feel the contractions we wouldn't push as hard.

"No, no, no!" I sobbed. "I'll push! I promise I'll push! At least let me try to push with the epidural, and if I'm not pushing well, then you can take it out. Please!"

She took one look at my tear-streaked face and agreed to let me try. I began pushing at 10:55 p.m., and after two pushes I asked the nurse if I was pushing well enough.

She looked at me skeptically and said, "Take your time, honey, it's your first. First babies take a while to come; you'll be pushing for at least an hour. I'm sure this baby won't come until after twelve."

After twelve? I had already been there for eighteen hours and I was exhausted. There was no way I would last another hour! I looked her dead in the eye and said, "No." I continued to push as hard as I could, pushing three to four times with every contraction, ignoring the doctor's orders to pace myself. After three more contractions, I was so worn out, I needed a minute to breathe.

The doctor informed me that with one more push

the baby's head would be out. "Come on, honey," he said, "he's right there. One more!" But I was done.

"I need a minute," I whispered. "Just one minute." I leaned back and closed my eyes as the room went silent. Everyone was waiting on me. As I laid there, I began to replay the past three years. Visions of negative tests and empty ultrasounds filled my mind. I forced myself to remember. I forced myself to see it all one last time. I saw the blood that flowed with each of my miscarriages. I saw myself lying on the bathroom floor crying. I saw myself in the doctor's office and heard his final words, "I don't know what is wrong." I felt, for the last time, the pain of shattered dreams, then I opened my eyes, looked at my husband and said, "Let's do this." The memory of my pain was all that I needed to grant me the strength to push.

Finally, I was here. Finally, I was a mom. With one hard push, his head was out, and then came his body. Just five minutes after I was told it would take two hours. I vaguely remember my mother and husband saying, "He's here, Jai! He's here!"

"Can I see him? Let me see him," I cried as the doctor held him up for me to see. That moment when I first laid eyes on my son is the one moment in my life that I will never forget. It is the single greatest moment and triumph of my life. A moment that is engraved on my heart and will always be until my very last breath. The first time I saw my son, it was like I had been missing him my whole life.

I have always believed that Christ died on the cross for my sins; I never doubted it. But a love so great that someone would die such a horrible, horrible death for me? That I could never understand. Not until that very moment when I first laid eyes on my son. All of a sudden, I felt it. I felt that kind of love that would cause one to give up their life for another. Because I would. For him.

Now I know that every mother feels this way, but I had never seen a more perfect baby. Holding him for the first time was like magic. I felt as though I could hold him forever. I was exhausted. I was ecstatic. I was hungry!

After we were moved into the recovery room, the real fun began. I was met by a nurse asking me how the pain was, if I needed drugs.

"Drugs?" I replied. "I'm not feeling any pain."

"Okay, I'll check back in an hour."

Her response scared me. Was I supposed to be in pain? My epidural had not yet worn off. And I was wondering what I should expect when it did. Would it be painful? Would it feel weird and empty? Well, let me tell you, the word *pain* doesn't even begin to describe what I felt as the sun rose that morning. I jabbed at the button on my bed rails frantically, until I heard a crackly voice. "Ready for the drugs, are ya?" She quickly appeared and delivered my relief.

After I gulped down the two Advil capsules and two Tylenol tablets, the nurse informed me that I was to let her know when I had a bowel movement. I gave her a strange look and asked why. I wasn't used to reporting my poops to anyone. Ladies, have you ever heard of the 'post-partum poop'? If not, let me tell you, the struggle is so, so, so very real.

You see, as the baby moves through the birth canal, everything it hits on the way down gets bruised. So afterward, peeing, pooping, passing gas, breathing, coughing, pretty much anything that adds a little pressure, adds a ton of pain. And every time I tried to pee, I was painfully reminded of how swollen my 'area' was. It felt like it was tripled in size and, I have to admit, I was curious to find out if it actually was tripled in size. So one morning, while both baby and daddy napped, I grabbed the pocket mirror I had stashed in my bag and made my way to the washroom. Let me tell you, after delivery you won't look the same down there. At least not for a while. But in the meantime, don't do it. Don't take the mirror down there. Oh, and do stock up on panty liners, because once you push that baby out, your bladder will never be the same. You'll pee yourself daily. Every time you sneeze, cough, laugh, take a deep breath, raise your voice, sit down, stand up, or bend over.

After a four-day stay in the hospital, due to a trip to the NICU caused by low blood sugar and a touch of jaundice, we were finally on our way home with our beautiful baby boy, Alex. As we drove home, I thanked God, over and over again. We were finally here. A family.

Chapter 8

One morning at about 4:30 a.m., I was awake feeding Alex, who has a very big appetite. When he was finally full, I lifted him to my shoulder for one last burp, when I realized that his diaper was full and his shirt was wet. After waiting so long for him to fall asleep, I knew that a diaper change was sure to wake him up. Reluctantly, I carried him to his change table and quickly changed his diaper and onesie. I then sat down to rock him back to sleep. As he drifted off, I found myself staring at his face, studying his little nose and his little mouth, when suddenly he opened his eyes and met my gaze. A slow smile crept across his sweet face before he closed his eyes again and drifted off to sleep. It was late and I was tired, but at just that moment I couldn't imagine that there could be anything in life more wonderful than this.

Now, I can't say that the fear of losing my baby ended with a healthy birth. After Alex was born, I often found myself fretting over his safety and the many pitfalls that awaited him. I tried not to worry too much as I enjoyed motherhood, and most of the time I was able to stop my imagination from running wild with possibilities—any mother worth her salt can easily drum up a lengthy list of the many, many ways her baby can be harmed—but still they remained tucked away in the back of my mind, ready to show themselves whenever the opportunity presented itself.

For example, when Alex was two months old, I attempted to begin the transition from sleeping in the bassinet beside me to sleeping in his nursery. He did so well. He slept soundly, waking only once a night for a feeding. What a champ! Then I got the email. On the second night, I received one of those automatic emails from a new mother's website warning of the risk of SIDS and spouting statistics of who was most vulnerable. It was an email sent with the sole purpose of terrifying me. Yes, me specifically. With widened eyes and a pounding heart I read the information. The risk of SIDS is higher between two to four months—Alex was two months old. And it was more common in black babies—his dad is black—who were born before thirty-seven weeks gestation—Alex was born at thirty-seven weeks and one day! *That falls within the range, doesn't it?* Of course, I opened it after having put him to bed and was instantly filled with a blood-freezing terror. My mind raced with images of me walking into the nursery in the morning to be greeted by the body of my precious baby, lying limp in his crib. Every twenty minutes, from then on, I was racing into his room to ensure that he was still breathing. By 3:00 a.m. I was exhausted and unable to fall asleep, because I was so afraid that my baby would die in his sleep. So I did the only logical thing. I prayed over my baby and went to sleep, knowing that God would take care of the blessing that He had given me, right? Of course not! I went downstairs to retrieve the bassinet that we had packed away and dragged it up the stairs to set it up, once again. I then announced to my husband that we will resume the transition in another two months, removed Alex from his crib, and placed him in his bassinet. Finally, I could sleep. Or so I thought. He was awake for the rest of the night, just to let me know how fine he really was.

As time went on, I became a little less paranoid. I hoped that I was only experiencing the same fears that all other mothers feel, regardless of their past. There are still times when I have to remind myself not to overthink and smother my boy, and it's getting more challenging as he grows older and less dependent on me. I know that in some small way those losses will always be with me. They show up in different ways, in different worries. As I've often mentioned, once you learn how quickly and easily someone you love can be taken away, you never really forget that lesson. But despite my past, I am learning that the best thing that I can do is present my worries to God in prayer and trust Him to answer. I am not strong enough to protect my children from all dangers, seen and unseen. And in this life, we all feel pain eventually. But I can pray that God will grant them the strength and courage they need to grow into the man and women that He has called them to be.

Although my pregnancy with Alex was healthy and rather uneventful, we still had no answers to the many questions we had when we were experiencing our miscarriages. What had caused them? If we didn't know what caused them, how could we prevent it from happening again? We knew that we wanted more children, but we didn't want to go down the same road to get them. So in January of 2015, when I found out that I was pregnant again, I was instantly filled with fear and anxiety, wondering what to expect this time around.

I'd like to say that the news of the pregnancy was met with joy and elation, but I can't lie. Alex was only nine months old, and we weren't expecting to have another baby so soon. I was scared. I knew that after everything we had gone through, I should have been ecstatic. Who cares if I didn't feel ready for another baby so soon? I didn't feel as though I had the right to complain; and boy, did I feel guilty. I had prayed and prayed for children, and now that I was pregnant with my second baby I was anything but the happy I should have been. I worried about introducing a new baby to Alex when he was still so young. Would he be jealous? How would we afford another baby? I had just started a new job, and already I would have to take maternity leave. What will my new boss think of me? And what about the baby? Will this pregnancy end in a miscarriage like the first six? If it did, would I be relieved? I was truly a mix of emotions. All I could say was, "Lord, you know best."

At about seven and a half weeks pregnant, my doctor sent me for a dating ultrasound. She wanted to be sure of the baby's progress, given my turbulent history. But the scan revealed some terrible news. The embryo was dating at five weeks gestation instead of seven, and appeared abnormal. I was told that it looked like either an abnormal yolk sac, a deformed embryo, or conjoined twins. However, since it was dating two weeks behind, they concluded that the baby hadn't been developing properly and had miscarried, but that my body hadn't gotten the message to release it, otherwise known as a *missed miscarriage*. I was told to go home and wait a few days for my body to 'get the message' and begin the miscarriage on its own. And as I left the doctor's office, I felt numb. How could I process this loss when I hadn't even had time to figure out how I felt about the pregnancy to begin with? I guess I had no choice but to go home and wait.

A few days after the results from the scan came in, I started spotting. Just a little in the morning, but it stopped by the time I got to work and didn't begin again all day. Nevertheless, I knew that this was it. Another miscarriage. I told Steven that perhaps this was God's will. We weren't even sure we wanted another baby so soon, so maybe this was for the best. I kept telling myself this over the next few days as I waited for the miscarriage to happen. I had no choice. Somewhere along the line, despite my fears and insecurities, I had fallen in love with that baby, and now I was losing it. I had to tell myself something so that I wouldn't fall apart. How could I have not been excited? How could I have ever doubted that I would want this baby? The guilt was overwhelming. I kept telling myself that I wasn't happy at first and now I was losing it, so I was getting what I deserved.

After two weeks, I still hadn't miscarried, and the guilt and sadness were so heavy on me that I was unable to eat and felt sick to my stomach. My doctor advised me to book a DNC in the coming week, but wanted me to go for one more ultrasound first just to see how things looked before my appointment. I reluctantly agreed. By this point I just wanted to be done with the whole thing. I called immediately and booked the scan for the next day, with the DNC booked for the following week. But God had another plan.

Chapter 9

The next day as I drove to my ultrasound appointment, I began talking to God and asking why this was happening again. If this baby wasn't meant to live, then why did I get pregnant? Why couldn't my baby have lived? I may not have felt ready, but I knew that God would provide for us. Didn't He always? As I prayed I began to cry. I didn't want to lose this baby. All of my fear and insecurity seemed to vanish into thin air as I begged God to please, please perform a miracle and save our baby!

I arrived at my appointment with a very heavy heart, grief and loss weighing me down. I had told my husband not to come. At the time, I felt it was unnecessary to have him there just to catch a view of my empty uterus and hear that we could go ahead with the DNC. But as I laid back on the bed for the scan, I wished that he was there holding my hand. I closed my eyes and tried to drown out the voice of the perky technician, who obviously had no idea how difficult this was and how desperately

I was trying not to cry in front of her. "Oh!" she exclaimed, in a super high-pitched voice. "Twins!"

I will never forget that day, that ultrasound, those words. I will always remember myself calmly informing the technician that we were not expecting twins and explaining why I was there and that we had a DNC scheduled for the following week. "You have the wrong file, that's not me."

She quietly listened, then turned the screen to face me, "Look," she said. "Two babies. It *is* you."

I slowly looked up at the screen, and there they were. *Two* babies. My babies. Alive babies. Separate and healthy.

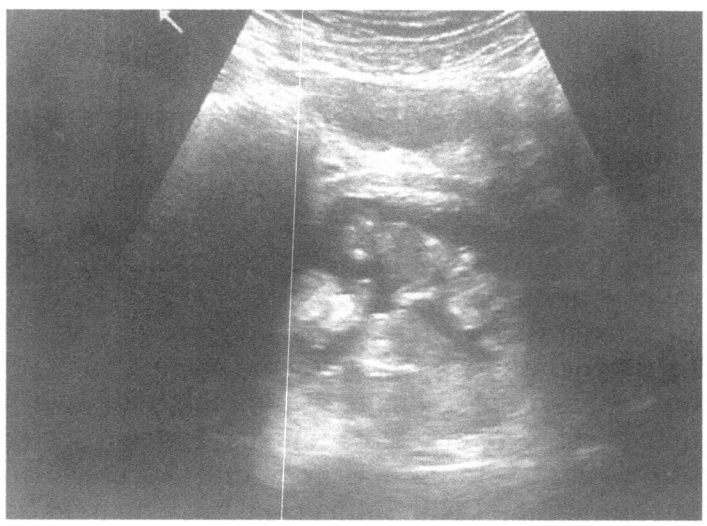

Our identical twin girls were born on August 31, 2015. Alisha and Alivia are two more living testaments of God's unfailing love for us, just like their older brother. Their very existence gave Steven and me the renewed ability to dream big and to act in faith, without the fear of failure. We *can* because we know that God will see us through. We have the proof three times over!

I often think about my younger self. I remember that little girl writing in her journal that she wanted to grow up and become a mother to a little boy and identical twin girls, just like in the Sweet Valley Twins. How grateful I am, today, that my big God heard the prayers of a small child and made her wildest dreams come true.

Nowadays I'm not as anxious about parenting as I used to be. I can feel safe trusting God every day to protect and watch over my babies. Without Him, without them, and without our story, I wouldn't be who I am today.

Chapter 10

When I was younger, writing a book was something that I always thought I'd like to do but never something I thought I could or would do. Then this season came along, and I thought that it was the worst thing that could ever happen to me. But God is so good! This experience that I thought was the worst thing that could have happened, this season that I thought would kill me showed me that I could do things that I never thought I could do. It showed me a warrior and a survivor inside of me that I never knew existed. It changed me for the better. As horrible as it was, I'm better because of it.

It doesn't matter how many times I tell people that I'm the mother of three kids under the age of two, the response is still the same, "You've got your hands full!" As true as that statement is, it is never said in a positive light, but with an undertone of pity, as though my life ended when one child suddenly became three. But the people who believe this don't really know, and how could they? Our children are my greatest blessing and my daily reminder of God's redemptive love. Every time I look at them I am reminded of just how much God loves us. Their very existence teaches me, daily, to wait on God. They are three beautiful miracles. They are my living testimony, my hope for the future, and my daily inspiration. Because they live, I cannot deny that God hears and answers prayer, and that He also lives.

There were times when I wondered if I had done something to deserve the losses that I suffered. Maybe I just had to suffer a little because, truthfully, I've done some unpleasant things in my life. In fact, if you ask me, I'd tell you that I probably deserve no better than what I got! Romans 6:23 says that "the wages of sin is death," and although the verse goes on, most people just stop there. We live a life ridden with guilt and condemnation, believing that we deserve the worst because of our sins.

When I was sixteen, I had a dream that was so vivid and real that I will never forget it as long as I live. In the dream, I was present at the crucifixion of Christ. I was robed in biblical attire, and was crying hysterically as I watched the soldiers nailing Christ to the cross. I knew that this horrible sentence was meant for me, and I begged them to kill me instead. The love I felt for this condemned man who was taking my place was so real, and it was killing me to see Him in my place. I clawed at the soldiers' backs and screamed at them to stop. I threw myself over Him trying to shield Him, but they were so much bigger and, with one hand, I was cast aside as they lifted the cross to stand. I felt so defeated as I knelt at the foot of His cross and wept, His blood pouring down and pooling around me. But at the end of the dream I looked up into His eyes and He said, "This is for you."

That dream showed me the extent of God's love for me. Of all the people on this planet who have ever existed, who exist today, and who will ever exist, if I was the *only* one to believe, He would have paid the same price. He would have died, even if it were just for me. And the truth remains that He would have died if it were just for you, the one reading these words. The point of the cross is that we don't have to feel guilt over the things we have done. Instead we can rest in His grace knowing that we are loved because Christ's blood covers our sin. We shouldn't feel guilty or afraid that we are being punished for things we have done, believing that we are getting what we deserve. Although the Bible does say that the wages of sin is death in Romans 6:23, it goes on to say that "the gift of God is eternal life through Christ Jesus our Lord." You see, that means that God didn't send His Son to die to bring justice to mankind. He sent His Son to die to *save* us from justice! What we deserve, He got. And that's not justice; that's grace.

God's grace covers a multitude of sin, mine and yours. I want to encourage you today, if you are struggling with infertility or pregnancy loss, to tell yourself that there is *life* in your womb. The Giver of Life is alive and well, and in His time your dream will be realized. So when you feel low, and you will, whisper the words, "There is life in my womb."

Epilogue

It is very unfortunate that infertility is one of the least discussed struggles, yet so many couples are struggling with it on a daily basis. Married women are asked so often when they would like to have kids that it seems to be believed that infertility is just a myth. Rarely do individuals take the time out to consider the fact that the person they are questioning may be having trouble getting pregnant, or may have even suffered a pregnancy loss. I remember being asked so many times when we were going to try for a baby and wanting to scream "I *am* trying!" I would dread going to family events, weddings, or baby showers, because I knew that there would be someone there who would pop the question and I didn't want everyone to know that I was broken, because that's what it felt like. I felt like I was defective, and I was embarrassed to admit it.

There is so much shame around not being able to have a baby, especially in this world where we expect our bodies to simply operate the way they were meant to. After all, infertility isn't exactly a sickness. It just means something is wrong, and it made me feel 'all wrong,' like I wasn't put together properly. Infertility doesn't show outwardly; it's like a secret shame. I would smile and tell people that we weren't in a rush, while fighting off the embarrassment I felt every time I was asked about having kids. The questions were a constant reminder of my deficit. They seemed to shout "Broken! Broken!" and I was pleading "Fix me! Fix me!"

My husband didn't have it any easier. A lot of times, as women, we forget that men are also greatly affected by their spouse's struggle to conceive. It is a man's natural instinct to want to protect his wife from pain, so watching her struggle and being unable to fix the problem can be quite challenging for a man to deal with. How does he answer those same questions and protect his wife's integrity? Where is the space for him to discuss his feelings about his wife's infertility? And what if he is the reason why they are having trouble conceiving? Up to fifteen percent of couples will experience infertility, and out of that half of the cases are due to male infertility. Consider the magnitude of this man's burden! When a couple is dealing with infertility, it is naturally assumed that the woman is the cause, so in many cases where the husband's infertility is playing a lead role, the wife still tends to feel the same shame. But whether it is the man or the woman who is experiencing infertility, both parties feel the burden equally. Ladies, we may not think that our men feel the pain as strongly as we do, but trust me, have a heart-to-heart conversation with your husband and you may be surprised by what he reveals. Most men tend not to talk about their feelings towards infertility, because they don't want to make their spouse feel worse about the situation but, when asked, they have a lot to say.

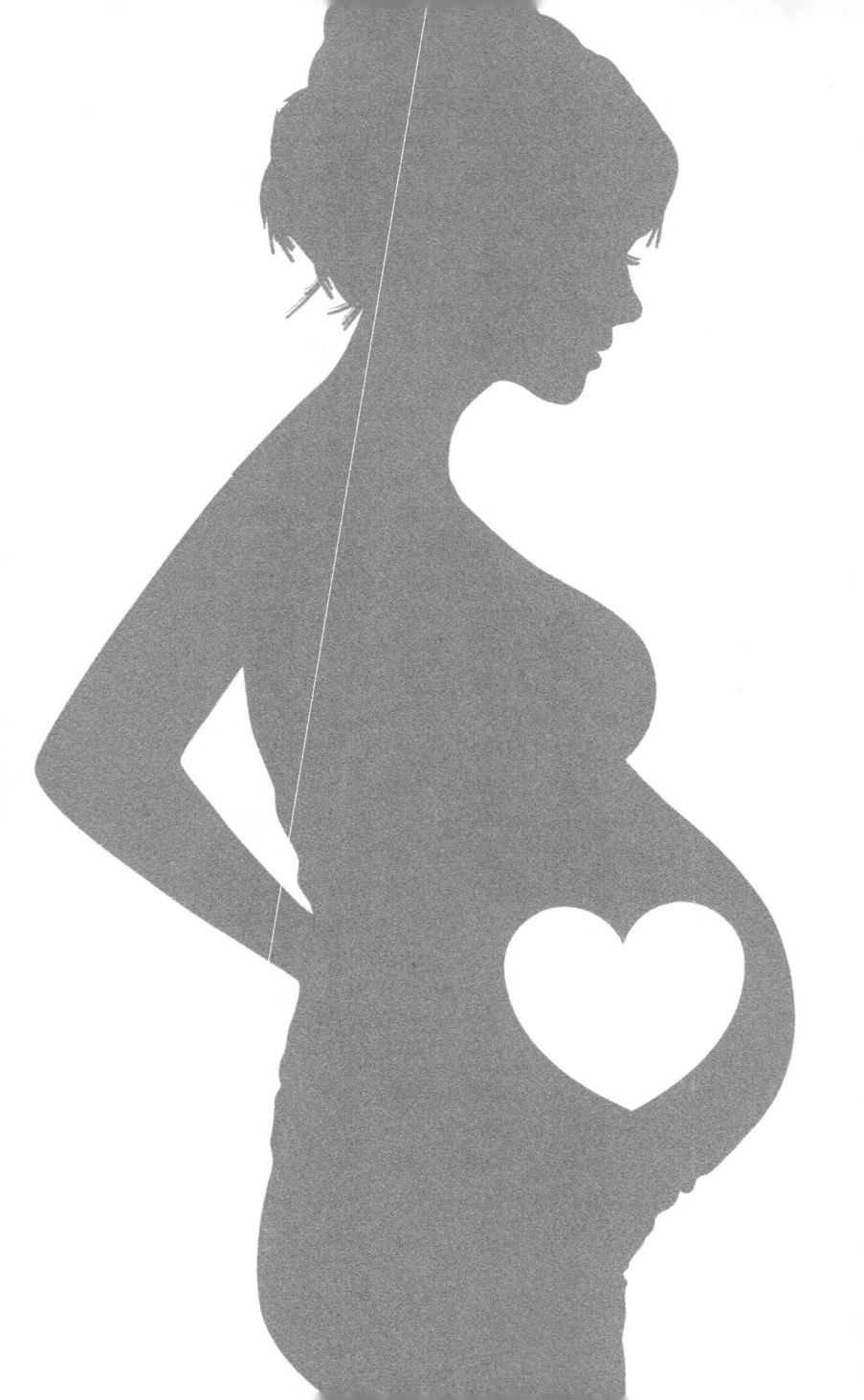

A Prayer for Your Womb

Dear God,

I thank You for Your unfailing grace towards me. I pray today that You will heal my heart and strengthen my spirit.

Lord, grant me courage and patience as I wait on You. Help me not to be disheartened when I feel as though the wait is too long and the road is too hard.

Today I choose to stand strong and believe that You have my best interest at heart. I will follow where You lead me, because Your plans are perfect. Renew my strength daily as I wait on You. Help me to remember that You are the giver of life, and that there is life in my womb.

Amen.

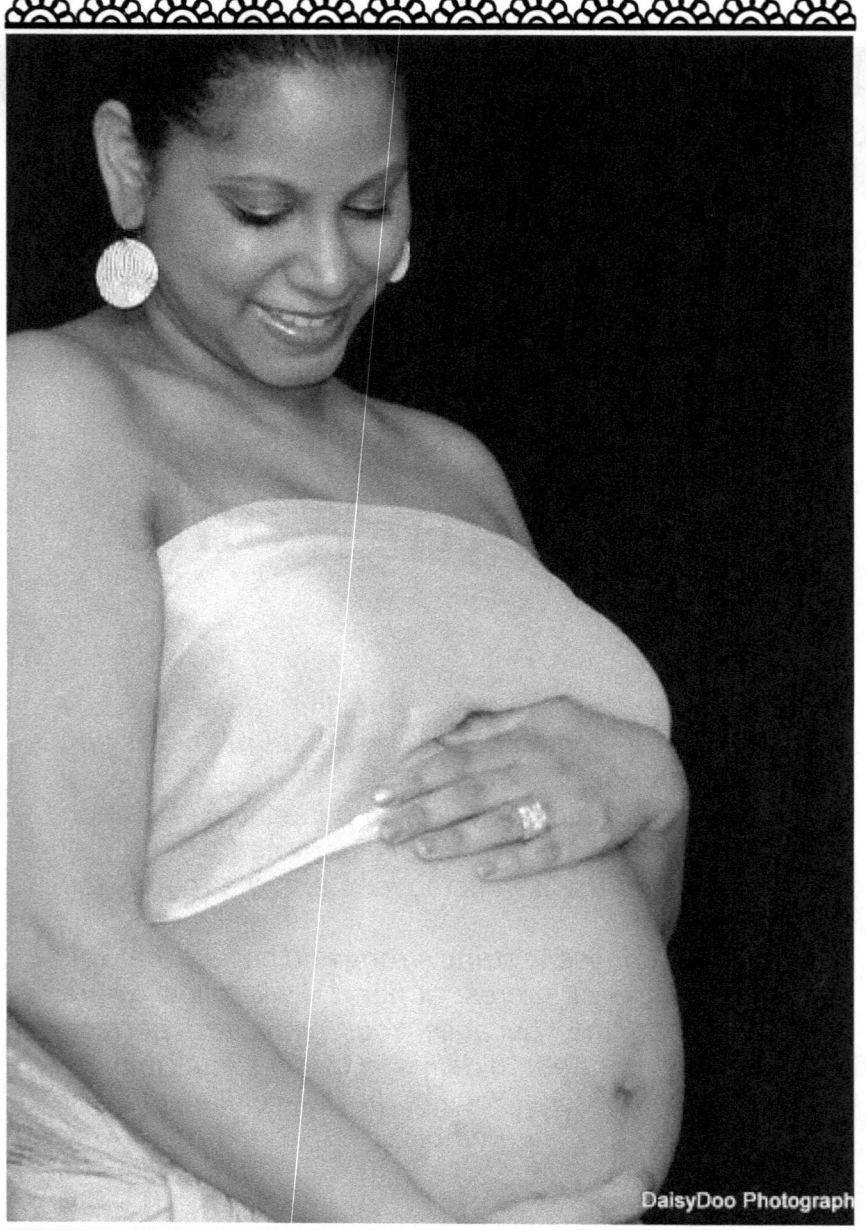

About the Author

Judine Gordon is a dedicated kindergarten teacher, wife, and mother. After years of struggle with infertility and pregnancy loss, she has made it one of her personal aspirations to encourage women everywhere who are facing a similar struggle. Judine and her husband, Steven, currently live in Ontario, Canada, where she spends her days looking after their three beautiful children.

www.ingramcontent.com/pod-product-compliance
Lightning Source LLC
Chambersburg PA
CBHW060208050426
42446CB00013B/3024